DARN IT ALL

Cindy Lowrey

ISBN 978-1-63814-217-1 (Paperback)
ISBN 978-1-63814-218-8 (Digital)

Covenant Books, Inc.
11661 Hwy 707
Murrells Inlet, SC 29576
www.covenantbooks.com

But we have this treasure in jars of clay to show that the surpassing power belongs to God and not to us. We are afflicted in every way, but not crushed; perplexed but not driven to despair; persecuted, but not forsaken; struck down, but not destroyed; always carrying in the body the death of Jesus so that the life of Jesus may also be manifested in our bodies. For we who live are always being given over to death for Jesus' sake, so that the life of Jesus also may be manifested in our mortal flesh.

—2 Corinthians 4:7–11 (ESV)

When peace like a river attendeth my way, when sorrows like sea billows roll, whatever my lot, thou hast taught me to know, it is well, it is well, with my soul.

—"It Is Well with My Soul," Philip Bliss

I feel blessed to be able to share my story. I have learned that God never makes mistakes, and he is always with me. My story does not start under the best of circumstances. So let's start at the beginning.

My dad's name was William Joseph Strong. He was born on July 7, 1939. His parents (my grandparents), Charles and Frances, had a tumultuous relationship. My grandmother was a model. She was beautiful. My grandfather was an alcoholic. He beat my grandmother constantly. The women in the family would take turns staying with my grandmother during the day so she would not get beat. As soon as they would leave, my grandfather would start beating her. Things just got worse. My grandmother received very bad advice from one of the women in the family.

She said, "Frances, if you want to stay married to Charles, you need to join him." So that is what she did. She began to drink and soon was an alcoholic herself.

When my dad was thirteen, his parents would take him to the bars as their drinking buddy. He was an alcoholic by the time he was eighteen years old. They lived in a low-income housing community in Warminster, Pennsylvania, called Lacey Park. Lacey Park is still there. In fact, if you drive on Jacksonville Road, you would pass the field behind the house we lived in.

My mother's name is Marlene. She was born on August 12, 1939. Her parents, oma and opa, Louise and Ernst, lived in Germany until my mother was about twelve years old. During the war, they saw their home being bombed two times. My grandfather had about seventeen dollars to his name when he, along with his wife and two daughters, Rosemary and Marlene (my mother), came to America. He became a barber. He built a home in Huntington Valley, Pennsylvania.

Grandfather Strong   Grandmother Strong

Grandfather Strong later years   Grandmother Strong later years

Buchholz Family

Grandmother Strong modeling

Mother and Father Wedding

For you formed my inward parts; you knitted me together in my mother's womb. I praise you, for I am fearfully and wonderfully made. Wonderful are your works; my soul knows it very well.
—Psalm 139:13–14 (ESV)

God made me. He made me for a special reason. It took many years for me to understand this but let us see how he works. Even though my siblings were born in the same mess I was, it affected each of us differently. Here is my story.

My parents met and started dating and were expecting their first child when they were sixteen. Debbie was born when they were seventeen. They had six children by the time they were twenty-four: Debbie, Mary, Nancy, Myself, Billy, and Marlene.

March 1, 1960, was the day I was born, Cindy Lou Strong. Our house was not a house full of love. My dad drank all the time. He would beat our mother and burn her with his cigarettes. He would take us on walks in the field behind our house and pick wild potatoes and wild asparagus with us. This was a pleasant memory of my dad doing something with us. I remember at one point our mother putting music on and dancing with us. I do not remember her saying she loved me. I do remember one night someone threw a rock through the window. It woke me up and I was scared; she let me lay on the couch with her until I calmed down. Other than that, I remember her being absent.

We hardly had any furniture in our house. Our house had two bedrooms. My parents had one room. We kids had the second room. Five of us would sleep on the bed, and my dad put a drawer on the floor with blankets in it for Marlene. She was just a baby. I was three years old at this time. There was hardly any food in the house. I remember there were many bugs in the house. Sometimes my dad would put beer in our bottles because there was not any milk. We did not have much clothing and would sometimes only have underpants to wear.

We would go outside by ourselves to play. There would be a group of boys in the neighborhood that would always make fun of us. We had a little dog named Poochie. Our dad found him and brought him home. Poochie would always follow us. One day when we were outside with Poochie, the boys came over and started making fun of us. They started throwing rocks at Poochie. We could not get them to stop. We carried Poochie home and he crawled under our bed and died. Needless to say, we were very sad and brokenhearted. I remember one night while we were all sleeping, our dad came home drunk. He came into our bedroom and took off his belt and started beating us. We woke up crying, jumping on the bed in hopes of getting away.

He did not beat Marlene. I was only three when this incident took place. I remember our dad being the parent that was home. I do not remember our mother at home much. While we were sleeping one night, she left. She left in the middle of the night. She was just gone. Our dad would have his buddies over and they would drink and get drunk. Our grandmother spoke with the other women in the family and said, "We have to get those kids out of that house." The six of us were divided amongst the family.

My sister Nancy and I went to live with our Aunt Jeanne and Aunt Margie. I do not think they liked having us. They would tell us to sit on our hands and not talk. They would tell us to go to bed and not get up until we found pennies under our pillow. We never found pennies. This arrangement did not work long. Our father didn't give any financial support, so the family didn't want us. Our dad took us to the Guardian Angel Home. This home was part of Catholic Charities. I was only three years old at this time. This was a very abusive home. We slept in large metal cribs. We were given a small receiving blanket. I remember always being cold. When we would sleep, I would lie on my stomach with my bottom in the air. The blanket would cover most of me that way. I would cry and rock myself to sleep.

One day I was very sick. At dinner that day, they gave us ice cream for dessert. I had a fever and threw up in my ice cream. I was crying and they told me to be quiet and eat every bit of my ice cream including the vomit. I ate every bit—I had to. I had no choice. We left this home because our mother came back and said she wanted to take us to live with her and her boyfriend.

She took us to an empty house. Our mother was always occupied with her boyfriend. We would sit together huddled on the floor. She would tell us to open our hands and pour carnation powdered milk in our hands. That was our main diet. A couple of days later, she said she had to go somewhere and was taking us to a friend's house. She would be back in a couple of days to get us. We were told to call her friend "Lady." She had a daughter our age. She had tons of toys, but we were told not to touch them.

Marlene was put in a high chair all day and would get slapped when she would cry. Our mother never came to pick us up. Child welfare was called and we became wards of the state because of child abandonment. We were all separated again.

I remember standing inside the Doylestown Courthouse watching strangers take my siblings away. They all were taken except Debbie and me. We stood there holding hands. A social worker came over to us with a man and a woman. They smiled at us and said they were taking us home with them. They looked nice but who are they? They were Peter and Angie Costanzo. We drove to a charming stone house in Glenside, Pennsylvania. We walked inside the house, and guess what—there was furniture. There was an unfamiliar smell, a good smell that made me hungry. They took us in the kitchen and we had our first spaghetti dinner ever. Of course, we had spaghetti because our foster parents were Italian. We shared a bedroom and each had a bed. I cried a lot. My foster mom would put me on her lap and Debbie would say, "Don't cry, Cindy. They will love us." You know that is all we wanted. To be loved. To be wanted by someone. We were just kids. Why weren't we loved? Why did everyone get tired of us and just throw us away?

Cindy and Debbie with	Cindy and Debbie with
their foster father	their foster mother

For the first time, we were shown unconditional love. Our foster parents were lovely people. I was four years old at this time. We also went to the doctor for the first time. That was when we found out I had malnutrition. I had to have all my baby teeth pulled. My baby teeth were all rotten because we had never eaten properly. Debbie went to school. I would go on walks and do a lot of shopping with my foster mom. They were very loving to us. They had an older son. They always wanted a daughter and now they had two.

I remember the first Christmas we had with them. Christmas Eve was spent at a foster relative's house. There were so many people there, laughing and having a wonderful time. We woke up to a lot of presents under the Christmas tree. One day when my foster dad was working, my foster mom received a call. She was told that my dad would be there by the end of the day to pick us up. We were going to a children's home with Mary and Nancy. We were to be packed and ready to go by that evening. My foster mom and foster brother cried all day. I did not know what was going on. Then a car pulled in the driveway. We got in the back seat. We just stared at Mary and Nancy. We did not know them. We had been separated for eleven months.

Our dad was in the front seat as his girlfriend drove. My dad never had a driver's license. We drove up to a huge stone house. We were at the children's home.

I would like to take a moment now and just pause. I have been asked many times as to why something like this would happen to us. We were just little kids. We were not the ones who were a mess—it was our parents. Psalm 68:5 (ESV) says, "Father of the fatherless and protector of widows is God in his holy habitation." It says that God is the father of the fatherless. I want you to know that is the absolute truth.

We were born by two people, but we were parentless. Our mother and father chose themselves and their lifestyles over us. They loved themselves more than they loved their children. Looking back, I do believe that God was teaching me the importance of family. I love my siblings. We stuck together. We had each other. There were no adults (except my foster parents) who cared about me.

So here we are again, being dropped off at our sixth placement. I was only five years old. Usually, you had to be six or going into first grade to live at this children's home, but my dad begged them to make an exception for me, and they agreed.

We walked in the front and were met by an older woman and a man with dark hair. The man told our dad to say goodbye. He said goodbye and left. The man with the dark hair was the director of the children's home. We called him Uncle Dick. The woman's name was Aunt Vera. She was our houseparent. We had to call everyone Aunt and Uncle. Aunt Vera took us to a big room full of children. My sisters and I clung together as we entered this room full of children we didn't know. We had been separated so many times and I thought it would happen again. A lady was leading a Bible club. She attended Davisville Baptist Church (which became the church we would attend). Her name was Aunt Vi. She explained to us that God loved us so much he sent his son Jesus to die for us on the cross. Three days later he rose from the dead. He forgives all our sins. He loves me and did this so we all could live with him in heaven forever. That was the night I trusted Christ as my Savior. Aunt Vi read a verse from the Bible that says, "For God so loved the world that He gave His only Son, that whoever believes in Him should not perish but have everlasting life" (John 3:16).

Did you read that? God loves the world, which includes me. My goodness gracious, *God loves me!*

Let the children come to me, and do not hinder
them, for to such belongs the kingdom of God.

—Luke 18:16 ESV

Behold children are a heritage from the Lord,
the fruit of the womb a reward.

—Psalm 127:3 ESV

God speaks many times in the Bible about children and the blessing they are. Even though I did not know or realize that yet, it would be a promise I would claim.

Let me take a little time to explain Bethanna to you. The proper name was *Bethanna, Christian Home for Boys and Girls*. It is located in Southampton, Pennsylvania. The property consists of forty some acres. There were four houses that provided the children with a bedroom and living room: one house for the girls (about ten of us) and three houses for the boys.

There was one house for the younger boys, one for the middle-aged boys, and one for the older boys. There was a house for the director and his family. About forty-five children were living there, while my sisters and I were there. There was a building that was called the barn. Many things were stored there. Clothes that were donated were stored there. There also was a trailer home where the cook and her husband lived. Behind our house was a small cottage where the nurse and her daughter lived. Our house was a large three-story house. It had a large enclosed front porch where everyone had a hook to hang their coats. The kitchen and dining rooms (where all of us ate together) were located on the first floor of our house. Also, on the first floor was our living room and a playroom. Our bedrooms and bathrooms were located on the second and third floor. There were many places outside to play. They even had a pool. Sounds like a nice place, doesn't it?

I want to make it clear—not every day was a bad day at Bethanna. Some children lived there and never had any abuse done towards them while at Bethanna. I am happy for them that they didn't have to endure that. Some of us were not as fortunate.

Before continuing with my story of Bethanna, I'd like to share some things the community did for us. Community groups would send us to Phillies games, Barnum and Bailey circus, and Crystal Cave, just to name a few. There would be a Christmas party each weekend in December given by Westinghouse, Johnsville Navy Base, Sears Department Store, and the Bell Telephone company. We would receive a new pair of shoes from Sears, and Westinghouse would buy each of us a new winter coat. For our birthday, the Bell Telephone Company would let us pick a gift out of a catalog. I picked my favorite doll one year, Mrs. Beasley. I loved her and would sleep with her every night.

Let us now begin with my story of my Bethanna years. Many who have heard my story would be sad for me. They would even tear up. Perhaps a good phrase would be "Darn it all." They would say, "Cindy, I am so sorry for what you went through. How did you make it?" It is bringing me great joy to share my story with you. If you look up the meaning of "darn it all," it will say "showing disappointment, sadness, and annoyance at a situation." However, another definition of the word *darn* is "to mend or fix." At the end of my story, I don't believe you will say "darn it all". I also think you will understand that it was not any person who mended or fixed my life, it was my Lord Jesus Christ.

All through those eleven years, God put people in my life that would encourage me to grow in my walk with Christ. Aunt Vera was one of them. I loved her and grew close to her. She would read the Bible with us every day. We had clean clothes, a bed to sleep in, and three meals every day. Our houseparent made Christmas a special time for us because we were the only family who had no family members who wanted to spend holidays with us.

There was a downside to living at the children's home. Within a couple of days upon arriving, we were given nicknames by the director, Uncle Dick, and some of the older boys.

The nicknames were used to make fun or put you down. I was five and did not have teeth; I was called tooth. When my teeth finally came in, I was called corn teeth because they were not perfectly white. When I got glasses in second grade, I was called four eyes. In sixth grade, I had a terrible complexion and was called "pizza face," or I would be asked, "Cindy, it looks like your face was on fire. Did someone put it out with an ice pick?" There was one name we were all called that was the most hurtful. We were all called Homer. I hated that name. Every time I was called that, it meant I lived at a children's home because my parents did not want me. Of course, I knew that but did not need to be reminded of it every day. We were even called *homer* at school. Kids would say, "She's a homer, her parents gave her away because they didn't love her."

Even though I was very young when this started, I started believing what I thought to be true. I believed I was unlovable. I mean, come on, not even my parents wanted me. I was now at a place where I would cry every time someone calls me a name. This was a Christian home. We were supposed to feel safe. I was a sad, scared child. My sisters and I have been separated so many times, and I always had the fear of that happening again. We had been rejected by family time and time again. I thought perhaps this rejection is normal because it was all I knew. Would we be rejected at Bethanna as well?

Uncle Dick had a terrible temper. He would beat us. Usually, it seemed to happen in the dining room when we were all eating. If one of the boys got in trouble at school, he would knock them off their chair, start screaming at them, and kick them in the side and stomach, sometimes even punching them in the face. Then he would hit the boy sitting next to the boy getting the beating and would say, "You too." One time the school called and reported that some of the boys misbehaved that day. While we were eating in the dining room that evening, he called those boys up and had them stand in a line.

He took off his belt and hit each of them. He did this in front of all of us. I was five or six at this time. I only remember being hit by my dad with his belt the one time he came home at night drunk.

Here Uncle Dick was whipping these boys and whipping them hard for all of us to see. One day, while we were eating lunch, his son did something that made him angry. He knocked him on the floor and was punching him and kicking him, and then he threw him through the screen door. Uncle Dick's wife didn't even say anything. When this would happen, I never understood why a houseparent would not stand up and tell him to stop. It was wrong. No one stood up for us. How could they just sit there and watch and not do anything? This created a tremendous fear in me toward Uncle Dick. When I would see him, I would get sick in my stomach.

The houseparents and staff would have meetings with Uncle Dick to discuss the kids and their behavior. While discussing me, concerns for me being very fearful of men were brought up. They treated this issue as something wrong with me. The issue was not me; it was the anger problem Uncle Dick had. Also, other male houseparents had very harsh ways of disciplining the boys who lived in their house. One houseparent would squeeze the pressure point on the boys' necks until they cried in pain. So yes, absolutely, I was very afraid of men. How could they not understand this? So I was treated as if I had the problem and not him. Yes, my fear of men became a big problem for me but not because of me or even my father. It was because of Uncle Dick and his problem. He was the root of my fear of men.

A few weeks after we arrived at Bethanna, school started. I was entering kindergarten at Shelmire Elementary School. I had a very nice teacher. I went to the morning session. I would ride the bus to school with the kids. Because I only went in the morning, there wasn't a bus to take me home. The school arranged for the tech school bus to drop me off. At that time of the day, the high school kids would get bussed to tech school. So it was a bus full of high school kids and me. They would make fun of me every day—I mean every day. They would tease me about my teeth or should I say lack of teeth except for the big one in the middle on top coming in. I would cry. The bus driver felt bad for me so he had me sit in the seat behind him.

When he would get to my stop, he would always give me a life-saver and tell me not to worry. He was very nice to me.

I did not care much for my first-grade teacher. From time to time, we would be given a reading test. I had trouble pronouncing some of my words. We would individually stand by the teacher's desk and read a long list of words out loud. I came to the word tail. I knew what it was, a tail on an animal, but could not pronounce it correctly. I kept saying, "tell or towel?" She got very angry at me and spanked me in front of the class. She wouldn't let me go to lunch with the class. She finally gave up and let me go. When I got to the cafeteria, the milk line was closed. My sister Nancy saw me crying and brought her milk over to me.

After recess, my teacher called me up to her desk to continue. I was so nervous. It took every muscle in my face, but I finally was able to say "tail." She made the entire class clap for me. I was humiliated. From that day forward, I hated school. I would even fake stomach-aches so the nurse would send me home.

Around this time, a couple, Uncle Chuck and Aunt Dede, came to work at Bethanna as the day-off replacement houseparents. They would take care of us when Aunt Vera had two days off a week. The first time I met them, I was at the bottom of our stairs. They were at the top. All I thought was, *He is the tallest man I ever saw, and she has a pretty smile.* They looked very nice. They had three sons. They brought their youngest son Jon because he was still in school. He was about four or five years older than me. He was funny and would always make us laugh. We met their other two sons shortly after they arrived—Mike, their oldest son, and his wife, Kaye; and Terry, their other son. I became very attached to them over the years. They cared and loved us very much. In years to come, they became very import-ant to me and became family.

When I was about twelve years old, Uncle Chuck and Aunt Dede Otto took me and my sister to Hershey Park for the weekend. Their son Jon came also. Jon always made us laugh and was fun to be with. It was a great weekend even though I got pink eye. We had a great time. It was special being away with my sisters.

A short time later, we were told that Aunt Vera would be retiring and we would get a new houseparent. This greatly upset me because I loved Aunt Vera very much. Just like being pulled away from my foster parents, Aunt Vera, whom I loved, would also be leaving me. I was seven years old at this time.

The day came when our new houseparent would arrive. Her name was Aunt Shirley. She knew Uncle Chuck and Aunt Dede. Uncle Chuck and Aunt Dede sent her a picture of my sisters and me. They told her we needed a houseparent to take care of us since Aunt Vera was leaving. She decided to come. I also loved her very much. It seemed when someone showed me love, I would get very attached to them. I just wanted to be loved.

My sisters and I knew how important it was to look out for each other and made it a point to do so. I became a very shy, quiet, fearful little girl. You could tell by my eyes. I had sad eyes. I did not like to be singled out for anything, even if it was for an accomplishment. I became pretty pathetic, at least that's what I thought of myself.

Our new houseparent was a wonderful person. She loved us very much. She encouraged us in our walk with the Lord. She would read the Bible to us every day. We sang in the kids' choir at church and went to pioneer girls. Over the years, she even took us to Ohio to visit her family, also Saturday shore trips, and even to Florida one summer. I always looked forward to Christmas, the week between Christmas and New Year specifically because my sisters and I would be the only children at Bethanna that week. Everyone else had family members who would want them to come home that week for the holidays. We did not have any family who wanted us. Aunt Shirley did things with us during that week to make us feel special. On Christmas Eve, we would go to church, come home, and have popcorn and hot chocolate in our Santa mugs. During this week, it almost felt like we were a normal family because it was just us.

In 1968 our caseworker told our houseparent that our brother and little sister wanted to come to visit. Because I was only three years old the last time I saw them, I forgot they were my brother and sister. Our sister was going to come live with us. Our brother had a wonderful foster family and would continue to live with them. If he did come live at the children's home, he would have to live in the little boys' house. We didn't want him to live there because that houseparent was mean. He had a foster family that loved him very much. He would be able to visit us once a month.

The houseparents would have meetings and discuss each child and what they thought we were going through and how to handle it. I'd like to share with you some of my evaluations with my input.

September 1968 (eight years old)

Cindy is frequently complaining of stomach discomfort, believed to be a reaction to the sudden loss of houseparent.

My stomach discomfort was a real thing. I was not faking. When Aunt Vera left Bethanna, I believed that another person I loved was leaving me.

Everyone I loved seemed to leave me. This was very real for me.

December 1969 (nine years old)

At last contact, their mother spoke of those at the home that were making her feel awkward and unwelcome. At the time she seemed to only call us in an attempt to obtain information on her husband. Father or his girlfriend has called Bethanna prior to the past six months when they wanted toys, clothes, or furniture for their house and son they had together.

I read this and thought what a shame that my mother felt awkward. Shame on her. She had six children and basically threw them away. She did not want the responsibility of being a mother.

October 27, 1971 (eleven years old)

> The director didn't think it was advisable for the girls to see their mother because she comes for a short time and then leaves everything in a turmoil. She is a very disruptive person. He stated that she was very upset about the children being removed from foster placement and placed at Bethanna because she was thinking of placement as permanent and would have preferred them to be in a foster home.

I believed she wanted us to remain in foster care so there would be less of an obligation to visit us. Then again that probably would not have mattered. I only recall seeing her about five times since she left when I was three. I was in fifth grade at this time. Down deep inside I started to face the fact that my own mother did not even love me. I started believing that I was unlovable. It became a daily realization for me.

September–March 1971

> Cindy was told that she was cuter without her glasses; and afterwards, when anyone looked at her, the child would put her head down and would not look directly at anyone.

I started to wear glasses in 1967 when I was seven. I was called four eyes and hated that. I never felt I was a cute little girl. The names I was called confirmed that. As I became older and was told if I didn't have to wear glasses or didn't have so many pimples I would be cute, I became more self-conscious. When I turned fifteen, it was said to me, "If you want to be cute like your sisters, you need to start wearing makeup." I started believing that if I'm not as pretty as my sisters, maybe I was adopted. As ridiculous as this sounds, this thought began to enter my mind (of course, my birth certificate says otherwise).

August 27, 1972 (twelve years old)

Mother is now remarried and both her and new husband are both employed. She did not wish any hindrance or block in this marriage and felt complete separation from her children was the best policy.

Again, this was another example of my mother choosing herself over her children. I started to accept the fact that she does not love us.

April 5, 1973 (thirteen years old)

Cindy's words and actions generally show the picture of a girl who is somewhat unsure of her own worth and capabilities. She is uncomfortable about having to express her own opinions. Instead, she allies herself closely with her sister, or her housemother, and thus avoids having to identify herself as a totally independent being.

At this point, feeling everyone who loves me would eventually leave me, I felt if I agreed with any of their suggestions, even to the point of liking what they liked, never disagreeing with them, then surely they would always love me.

April 9, 1975 (fifteen years old)

Cindy is a very insecure child and needs constant reaffirmation. She tends to feel that everyone else is better than her. There are frequent apologies for wrongs which she has never done. She seeks to be like the people she loves which is definitely advantageous. She does not seem to be pleased with herself although she does seek continual recognition from especially the other girls. A serious problem that the housemother relates is that Cindy does not think enough of herself compared to the other girls to the extent that Mr. and Mrs. Strong actually adopted her. Comparisons to appearances and expressions do not satisfy.

I started believing that God made some people who just will not amount to much and would not have much to offer. I wanted to protect my sisters and that is why I would admit to doing something I did not do. I did not want them to get in trouble. I would tell them all the time that I love them. I'm sure it may have annoyed them because I said it so frequently, but they never showed that. I would tell Aunt Shirley all the time that I love her. She would get upset and say to me, "I know you do, Cindy. Stop saying that!" At this point, I believed I was a pretty pathetic kid.

May 15, 1975 (fifteen years old)

Cindy was discussed briefly, and her identification with the houseparent (Aunt Shirley) was mentioned. She has a fear and avoidance of men. She is supposed to sit at the little boys' table at meals once a week with Uncle Fred (social worker).

I'm not sure at all who thought it a good thing for me to sit with ten boys at meals and that it would help me feel more comfortable with men. Quite strange, I would say. My fear of men came from Uncle Dick. I'd get sick to my stomach every time I would see him. He was the issue, not just with me, but with many of the other kids who had to face his anger. None of the houseparents ever stood up to him. He continued showing anger to many of us kids.

When I was about ten years old and we were swimming in the pool, Uncle Dick came over and asked me to come to him. I climbed out of the pool. He asked where my sisters Debbie and Mary were. I was cold and shivering and just wanted to get back into the pool. I told him they were out. I waved my arm toward the road. He back-handed me in the face and told me I was being disrespectful. I stumbled to keep my balance. Everyone in the pool was silent. Not a peep. He walked away and I went back into the pool. I went to my sister Nancy and started to cry. The next day I told Aunt Shirley I was sick and couldn't go to school. I begged her to let me stay home and she said I could. I stayed in bed all day. After the house parents and staff finished lunch, Aunt Shirley brought Uncle Dick to my room. I was numb with fear. He made me say I deserved what he did and made me agree that it didn't hurt. I just wanted him to leave my room and I was afraid if I stood up for myself, he would hit me again. I was so afraid of this man. I had reason to be afraid.

I do understand the need to evaluate each of the children, but I'm not sure those doing the evaluations were qualified to make conclusions. Constant rejection from my parents definitely played a major role in my insecurities. Another conclusion that could have been made but was not is perhaps the way we were treated at the children's home played a large part in my insecurities and very low self-image. We were not the ones who made wrong and selfish choices. Our parents did. We were treated as broken children who needed to be fixed. We were disciplined very severely most times. In our house, many times we were told to go pick a branch from a tree to be hit with as a consequence for misbehaving. I would pick the smallest one thinking it would not hurt. It did and would leave welts on my back, arms, and legs. We would call this getting the switch. The boys had a punishment that was called rocks. They would have two five-gallon buckets and have to fill them with rocks and carry it to the other end of the property and then return all of them. This would take all afternoon and sometimes into the evening.

As I've shared my story from time to time, a question has been asked of me. Have I ever been sexually abused? Yes, I have. The sexual abuse was not from staff but from some of the older kids. Three times this abuse happened to me. I was sexually manipulated for the first time when I was five years old. The other two times I was eight and nine. I was too afraid to say anything. These kids were a lot bigger than me, and I knew no one would believe me. I was afraid if I said anything, I would be separated from my sisters again. I couldn't bear the thought of that. I couldn't let that happen, we were all we had. This abuse ended when those kids left Bethanna.

When I was eleven years old, one of my sisters tried to commit suicide. She saw the medicine cabinet unlocked and ingested thirty-six aspirin. I remember hearing Aunt Shirley screaming. The director was called and came to our house. He was extremely angry. You would think 911 would be called to get my sister immediate help, but no. They decided to make my sister stay in bed to have the effects wear off. She did a lot of vomiting and drifting in and out of sleep, unable to hold any food or liquid down. We had a refrigerator in the hallway near my sister's room. I was standing next to it wanting to see my sister, but I wasn't allowed to. Why couldn't I see her? I was so worried. After two days of her being extremely ill, they decided to take her to the hospital. While at the hospital they set my sister up with an IV. She was very dehydrated. No one stayed with her, she was left alone. I'm sure you may be wondering why such a young girl would be driven to this. My sister was molested as a very young girl by boys in the neighborhood before our parents separated. That, along with how we were treated at Bethanna, and the ridicule we received with all the names we were called. It was relentless, I mean constant, being put down all the time. No wonder we had no self-esteem. The staff were so worried for this to get out into the community. What would people think? What happens if another placement was made for this family of five and the funding was lost for this facility? As I later learned, we were wards of the state which provided Bethanna with a large sum of money given to them monthly on our behalf. It was as if we were the "cash cow". It wasn't until many years later that state supported children became the norm. This was another reason for this incident to be hushed. Would people start to question what really led to this? The staff was so mad at my sister and she was treated differently because of this. Their attitude was one of, "How could you do this to us? What would people think of this children's home?"

Romans 8:31 (ESV) says, "What shall we say to these things? If God is for us who can be against us?"

Years ago, someone very dear to me sent me a beautiful handkerchief and said she wanted all my tears to go in that handkerchief. She wanted me to remember as it says in Psalm 56:8 (ESV) You have kept count of my tossing; put my tears in your bottle. Are they not in your book.

God loves us and holds all our tears. He is ready to roll up his sleeves and help us with whatever we are going through. I keep this card and handkerchief in my Bible.

I wonder how my sister would have been encouraged and felt loved if someone would have shared something like this with her. Despite all that happened to my sister, she has a very fulfilled life.

Even though I am the fourth out of 6 children, I just wanted to protect my siblings. I would be willing to take punishments for them. They certainly never asked me to, but I would have in a second. It is awful and heart wrenching watching a sibling getting beaten or mistreated.

I was so happy when my sister came home from the hospital. God truly protected her.

We had daily chores to do. I believe this was a good thing. It taught us the responsibility of taking care of what we have. Someone donated what we have and we should take care of our belongings. We got our clothes from the barn. I believe I learned to appreciate what we had. The girl's house was responsible for setting the tables at mealtimes. The dining room was at our house. We also had kitchen and hostess duties. We would clean the kitchen and walk-in refrigerator on Monday nights. We weren't allowed to do much cooking ourselves. (I believe this is why I love to cook and bake now.)

Every summer we were sent away for two weeks for camp. I hated this. It was another form of what I thought to be separation from my sisters. I would worry about them because we would not be in the same cabin or at the same camp because of our ages. I was at the same camp with two of my sisters. I would be so afraid I would cry until they let me be in the same cabin as Nancy. The fear of separation and rejection was a major issue in my life. The rule at the children's home was once you graduate from high school you had to leave. This always weighed heavily on me because my sisters and I had nowhere to go. I worried about what would happen to us.

As a little girl, I always dreamed of getting married and having a lot of children, living in a single home. When riding the bus home from school, I would lean my head against the bus window and watch as kids would get off the school bus and run to their houses. I would wonder if they would get a hug from their mom and dad. What would they talk about at their dinner table? What was it like? Would that ever be a reality for me?

When I was in seventh grade, I started to doubt my salvation. I felt so many people have said they loved me but would stop loving me or leave me. What if God did that. For two years, I doubted my salvation. I wouldn't smile. I completely lost my self-confidence so much that I started believing this was the way God made me so I should accept that. Maybe he made some people who were supposed to be worthless. I wanted to be a strong person. I wanted to be of worth to someone. I knew God created me and put me on this earth for a reason. I finally decided to stop relying on my feelings and to claim what God says in 1 John 5:13 (ESV): "I write these things to you who believe in the name of the Son of God, that you may know that you have eternal life." My doubts didn't just go away overnight. It truly was a process, a long hard process. Reading my Bible and having a consistent prayer life was key to my freedom from doubt.

In tenth grade, Aunt Shirley was fired. We found out that day when we came home from school. We went into her room to say hi to her, and there were boxes everywhere. She told us she was fired. I fell to the floor crying. We were told the director thought it wasn't good for her to be close to us. Why was it wrong for us to be loved by someone. He told her she shouldn't believe we loved her. He said those girls are going to end up like their mom and dad. That same fear of rejection came back. Darn it all! I felt another person whom I loved was leaving us. Aunt Shirley had taken care of us for seven years. Why? Did God have a plan?

A couple of weeks after she left, Uncle Dick called us in his office. He pointed his finger in our faces and said, "If you girls think anyone will ever want you, you're crazy. You will never be loved. You will never amount to anything. Everything you do will fail."

This made me very angry inside, but at the same time, I believed it to be true. After all, for the last eleven years, we were treated as if we were unlovable and broken, unable to be fixed.

Within a couple of weeks, my sisters and I met with our social worker, and she told us that Aunt Shirley wanted us to come live with her. She explained a lot had to be approved before this could happen but wanted to know if this would be something we would want. Of course, it was. Aunt Shirley loved us and we loved her. It took about two months. We got home from school one day and our houseparent told us we were going to live with Aunt Shirley. Uncle Dick told us to pack. He wanted us gone by the end of the following day. We were very excited. Finally, we would be a normal family living in an apartment. We packed all that we could. I remember having a Mrs. Beasley doll. She was that special doll I wanted to have forever. However, we had to hurry and pack in one night and I forgot to take her.

People from our church donated furniture for us. A family even paid our rent for several months. This was eleven years after entering the children's home. Were things beginning to turn around for us? I certainly thought so. I had a lot of healing to do inside. I needed to start trusting that God made me the way I am for a special reason. I am worth something. I am loved. It still took many years for this to be a reality in how I viewed myself. I needed to start claiming God's promises instead of relying on my feelings. I knew I did not want to become a statistic. I was determined not to let my childhood determine who I would be as an adult. I wanted to live for Christ.

Cindy age 3   Strong siblings

Cindy age 5

CINDY LOWREY

Cindy age 5

Cindy 1st grade

Cindy 2nd grade

Strong siblings with father

Cindy on the front of
Bethanna's Christmas card.

Cindy 3rd grade   Cindy 4th grade

Cindy and Nancy

Cindy

Cindy with Santa Clause

Debbie, Nancy, Cindy and Mary

Strong girls

Cindy 5th grade   Cindy 6th grade

Cindy and Marlene

Strong Siblings with mother

Cindy 7th grade

CINDY LOWREY

Cindy 16 years

Cindy 11th grade

Cindy senior picture

But they who wait for the Lord shall renew their strength;
they shall mount up with wings like eagles; they shall
run and not be weary; they shall walk and not faint.
—Isaiah 40:31 ESV

Lord, give me the strength to be who you want me to be. I always prayed I would one day have a husband and family I could love unconditionally. When asked what I wanted to be when I grow up, I simply would say, "I want to marry a special man and have children and live in a house." I would dream about this as a little girl; and the older I would get, it became something dear to me that I would pray about.

> The Lord Himself goes before you and will be with you; He will never leave you nor forsake you. (Deuteronomy 31:8 ESV)

> Be strong and courageous. The Lord your God will be with you wherever you go. (Joshua 1:9 ESV)

> The Lord God is my rock, and my fortress, and my deliverer; my God, my strength, in whom I will trust; my buckler, and the horn of my salvation, and my high tower. (Psalm 18:2 KJV)

Let me remind you of 2 Corinthians 4:7–11 (ESV):

> But we have this treasure in jars of clay to show that the surpassing power belongs to God and not to us. We are afflicted in every way, but not crushed; perplexed but not driven to despair; persecuted,

but not forsaken; struck down, but not destroyed; always carrying in the body the death of Jesus so that the life of Jesus may also be manifested in our bodies. For we who live are always being given over to death for Jesus' sake, so that the life of Jesus also may be manifested in our mortal flesh.

I knew God still had to do a lot of molding to make me the beautiful jar he wanted me to be.

We lived in an apartment with Aunt Shirley for a short while and then into a house that was larger for us in Huntingdon Valley. Believe it or not, it was a couple of streets from our oma and opa's house. Our mother came to visit oma and opa and also came to our house for a short visit. We hadn't seen or heard from her in years. We didn't know her. During this visit, she told us she has a new life now and we need to accept that. We all just responded with "okay." We just didn't know her and didn't know what to say. She never was a part of our lives. Why would this upset us?

Strong siblings with Aunt Shirley

Years later, I called the children's home and requested my records. There was a different director at this time. Usually when records are requested, the director goes through and pulls out certain papers. When I called for my records, he was away on vacation. The secretary pulled my records and gave me everything. I found a letter written by Aunt Shirley when I was fifteen years old. I'd like to share it with you.

Cindy came to the children's home when she was five years old. She has four other sisters here and one brother in a foster home.

She is very insecure. In her eighth grade, she doubted her salvation all the time. She kept coming to me and told me she needed to be saved. She even on her own went to our pastor, and he gave her verses to give her assurance. The next day she still came to me with her doubts.

In the past, on my day off, she would stand at her door or my door waiting to see if I would come out so she could say good morning to me.

She watches everything I do and even eats like I do. If I would say I like something, even if it wasn't good, she would say she likes it too. She tells me over and over again that I am her real mommy and that she loves me so much that she can't say it. She says she is sorry all the time even if she isn't the one that is wrong.

Even her sisters say, "Cindy, don't say you are sorry all the time." We could pass each other in the hallway and maybe hit each other; and right away she says, "I am sorry." I would say, "Cindy, you didn't do anything wrong."

She would act hurt.

She is so slow in doing things, like homework, cleaning, etc. I do things fast. I know I nag her in trying to get her to go faster. When she comes home from school, she tells me her whole day.

Every test and especially if she fails one. I always give the wrong reaction and get upset when she fails. I know she wants my attention.

She knows that she is supposed to do her homework before going anywhere, but the other night, I was taking the girls to ranch. After we got there, she told me that she didn't finish her homework.

She really drives me crazy. Before she got out of the car, I told her, "It better not happen again and I mean it." I know she needs so much praise.

When we are walking out to the car, Cindy will run up and take hold of my arm. No one else will even try. Even at the mall, she always has to hold on to me. Down deep, I want to run away.

At church, Cindy always has to sit by me. This is a while back. She even told me that she hadn't sat with me for ten Sundays. I had the younger ones sit with me. I told Cindy that I guess I would have to keep a schedule so she could have a turn. I asked her why she doesn't sit with young people her own age. She does sit with them, but always with her sisters. She doesn't have any friends. I mean close ones.

I have talked to Cindy many times. One time I said to Cindy, "Will you please forgive me for the way I treat you? I am sorry."

She said that I don't treat her bad but I only try to help her.

I don't know what to do because I feel so guilty with the way I feel about her.

Last week, I took her out to eat and talked to her. I told her that she was on level five and I am not going to bug her anymore about doing her homework. I know I had put her under pressure in getting her things done.

I told her that she could make her schedule out each week to get her work done. This would be just between the two of us. She is also a hostess on Saturday and kitchen girl on Sunday. I know Cindy feels better but that still isn't the answer. What should I do? I know she needs help, and I feel I can't do it.

I know I don't treat her the right way and I don't know why. She would ask me something and I would say no. But if one of the other girls would ask, I would probably say yes.

On Monday, she asked me if she could talk with me after she cleaned the walk-in refrigerator. I said yes. She came in and we watched TV. She said she just wanted to be with me.

I know I do not answer Cindy right. I know it is not all Cindy but my reactions toward her.

She needs so much encouragement.

She doesn't have any confidence in herself at all. When she apologizes all the time, she will get very upset if you don't accept it. She really thinks she is wrong.

I need help in dealing with Cindy.

She smothers me.

I was about forty years old when I read this letter. I started sobbing when I read it because I truly thought this person who wrote this letter loved me. I felt it portrayed me as this pathetic girl; but in all reality, I believed back then I was pathetic. You see, all I wanted was to be loved and wanted to give love. Isn't that what any child wants? I know growing up I had an unhealthy way of thinking. I felt if I agreed with everyone they would love me in return and want to be around me. Simple things like my favorite color, what I would decide as a hobby, and what food I like—every decision was what someone thought I would want. I didn't want to upset the person or cause friction, so I would agree with them. To be honest it worked in many cases. It is very hard to try to please everyone, but I believed that was how to get people to love me. I felt this way for so long I started accepting the fact that I wasn't the type of person that would be loved because of who I was. I just wasn't good enough to be loved. I felt I had to work for that love. I started believing that God created me to be someone who wouldn't be important enough and would always live in someone else's shadow. Growing up and until I met my husband, I lived in my sister's shadows. I was okay with that because I love them. I thought if I disagreed or spoke up for myself, they might get mad and not love me as much. To be honest, I became an adult with a very low self-image. I've always wanted to keep the peace. I wanted to please everyone even if it would be at my expense. This was not what God wanted me to be.

I will praise thee; for I am fearfully and wonderfully made: marvellous are thy works; and that my soul knoweth right well.

—Psalm 139:14 (KJV)

I knew this verse and understood what it was saying. God made me special, just the way he wanted me to be. He has a special plan for me. The thing is, I didn't feel that way in my heart. I had a head knowledge but not heart knowledge. I decided to trust God to show me the plans he has for me. I am not a victim. I have victory in Christ. It was about time for me to start living that way. There is no magic trick or quick fix to regaining confidence or knowing the value of yourself. I had to ask God constantly to show me my worth in him. It is a continuing process. Reading my Bible and praying are key to my life being changed.

We all have times when our confidence or self-esteem isn't where it should be. I know when that happens to me, I'm not trusting in the Lord. I need to continue seeking Him.

Psalm 119:18 (ESV) says, "Open my eyes, that I may behold wondrous things out of your law."

Cindy 22 years

It is the Lord who goes before. He will be with you; He will
not leave you or forsake you. Do not fear or be dismayed.
—Deuteronomy 31:8 (ESV)

For I know the plans I have for you declares the Lord, plans
for welfare and not for evil, to give you a future and a hope.
—Jeremiah 29:11(ESV)

It took a lot of rain to make a day like this. Grass is not
so green from blue skies and sunshine only. There have
to be whole days upon days of gray skies, wet parks, and
mud puddles. Children sitting indoors, waiting.
But on a day like this I can try to appreciate the rain.
Everything around me is green and clean and beautiful. Lord,
please help me to understand my rainy days as they come
and be grateful for them because of what they bring.
M. Otto

Darn it all? I don't think so.

Here's where my story gets really good. In fact, I have a smile on
my face as I am typing this. I met my husband in 1981. We met in
church. Before Michael started coming to our church, his brother Bob
and his wife came to our church. At one of our Wednesday night Bible
studies, Bob asked us to pray for his brother Michael. He said Michael
was making some bad choices and he wanted Michael to understand
what Jesus did for him on the cross. We prayed for Michael; and shortly
after, he trusted Christ as his Savior and began to change his life. He was
twenty-one years old. Bob told us Michael was going to start coming to
our church. I remember the first time I saw him. I was getting a cup of
coffee and turned around just as he walked by me. He caught my eye

(in a big way). He is very handsome. We started dating a little over a year later. Michael loved the Lord and that was very important to me.

Our first date was on his motorcycle. I always said I would never ride a motorcycle, but he was very cute, and I was waiting a long time for this to happen. Michael lived about thirty minutes away in New Jersey. From the first conversation I had with him, I knew he was a very kind man. Could this be, he accepted me for who I was. He wanted my opinion on things. He was interested in my feelings. He appreciated me. He loved me unconditionally. I couldn't believe that God had such an amazing man for me. Slowly but surely, I started coming out of my shell. My self-image and confidence started to grow. Remember the verse I shared earlier? Psalm 139:14 says, "I will praise thee; for I am fearfully and wonderfully made." Through a lot of prayer and reading my Bible, my head knowledge became heart knowledge. Michael never tried to change me. We would read our Bible together and encourage each other. We also would pray together. We grew closer and closer. I knew I could talk to him about anything. He became my best friend. What an unbelievable gift God has given me. I knew I wanted to marry Michael about three months after we started dating.

We didn't get engaged however until about one and a half years later. We were married on May 4, 1985. What a joyful day. I became Mrs. Michael Lowrey. I truly can't thank my Lord enough for Michael. He is all I prayed for and so, so much more. What a blessing and gift from God. God is good.

God is good all the time.

God gave us the most amazing children.

1984 engagement picture   May 4 1985 wedding day

Stephen was born on June 23, 1986. After Stephen was born we had a miscarriage. Thomas was born on July 12, 1988. Alissa was born on April 13, 1990, and Nadine, January 31, 1992. We have always had a house full of noise. Dinners around the kitchen table. Outside time, inside time. I always loved how our children would run to the door when their dad would come home from work. I loved watching the kids wrestle with their dad and jumping on him. I would put the kids to bed and I would hear a lot of noise. When I would go up to settle the kids down, I would find out that the noise was their dad jumping on their beds and shaking their mattresses. They would all be laughing so hard. One of the beds even broke because of that. These are precious times that will never be forgotten. As young children, our kids understood the sacrifice Jesus gave for them. They all accepted and understood what Jesus did for them through his death and resurrection. That was very important to Michael and me.

For God so loved the world that He gave His
only begotten Son that whoever believes on Him
should not perish but have everlasting life.

—John 3:16 (KJV)

I have always wanted to make sure my children knew how much their mom and dad love them. Being their parents is an awesome blessing. We are so proud and honored that they are our children. I honestly feel God has given Michael and me the best family imaginable.

Honeymoon fun   Family vacation 1993

Earlier on in my story, I mentioned I always dreamed of getting married and having a big family.

Thank you, Jesus, for this blessing.

Our children are all adults now. Michael and I are grandparents to the most precious grandkids ever. Boy, they just steal your heart every time you see them. As our family continues to grow, we want our children and each person in our family to know God has a plan for each of them.

Lowrey Children younger

Lowrey Children

Lowrey children older

I pray the legacy we leave will be one that brings honor and glory to God.

I will not ever know what it is like to have a mom and dad who love me. I don't know what it is like to be swooped up into the arms of my mom and dad as they whispered in my ear they love me. I do not know what it is like to have a mom and dad who cared what I would become. *That's okay.* I have a better blessing of loving my husband and four children and their growing families. I love showering my family with love. Would I go through my childhood again, you may ask? Absolutely, in a second. Look what God has given to that little sad girl.

I love my life. God is the reason I do. He had a plan for my life. Thank you, Jesus.

> When peace like a river attendeth my way,
> When sorrows like sea billows roll,
> Whatever my lot,
> Thou has taught me to know,
> It is well, it is well, with my soul ("It Is Well with
>   My Soul," Philip Bliss)

Great is your faithfulness, Lord, unto me.

I know there are many people today who have gone through much harder times than I did. I started as an unloved little girl. I don't hate my parents. I forgive them. A huge thing I had to learn to do was forgive. Ephesians 4:32 (NKJV) says, And be kind to one another, tenderhearted, forgiving one another, even as God in Christ forgave you.

That verse does not say have the feeling of forgiveness it says to forgive. I did not deserve Christ's forgiveness but He gave it to me anyway because of His love for me. There will be many people in our lives who won't ask for forgiveness when they should. We need to forgive them regardless. Not only is this a healthy thing to do, it keeps us from becoming bitter. My choice was to forgive because Christ forgave me. God took care of the feeling of forgiveness as time passed. My father passed away on May 13, 1990. My mother lives somewhere in Florida. I am honored God chose me to go through what I went through. Whoever is out there feeling unloved, broken, or scared, please know that God has a plan. He loves each of us unconditionally, with perfect love. He died for all of us and wants us to live in heaven with him. He sent his perfect son Jesus to die for us on the cross as payment for all our sins. "But God shows his live for us in that while we were still sinners, Christ died for us" (Romans 5:8 ESV). He didn't stay dead, he arose. "He is not here, for he has risen, as he said. Come, see the place where he lay" (Matthew 28:6 ESV).

This is a free gift to us. "For the wages of sin is death, but the free gift of God is eternal life in Christ Jesus our Lord" (Romans 6:23 ESV). We only have to accept his death, resurrection, and forgiveness. "Because, if you confess with your mouth that Jesus is Lord and believe in your heart that God raised him from the dead, you will be saved. For with the heart one believes and is justified, and with the mouth one confesses and is saved. For the Scripture says, Everyone who believes in him will not be put to shame" (Romans 10:9–11 ESV). I pray you accept that gift.

I want to share just a few updates. After about forty-seven years, I reconnected with my foster mom and foster brother and his family. My foster dad had passed away. I called and spoke to my foster

mom on a Tuesday, and we were at their dinner table that Sunday eating a spaghetti dinner. Remember earlier I mentioned that was the first dinner Debbie and I had with them when I was four. I put together a photo album and wrote a letter about my story since leaving their care.

I would continue having coffee with her once a week until her health failed and she lived in a care facility. Michael and I would visit her until she passed away at 104 years old. What a blessing she was to me.

Here is another blessing that happened a few years ago. When our mother left us, she had two more daughters from two different men. She put them up for adoption. Four years ago one of them found us. Her name is Barbra. She is six years younger than me. It is a blessing getting to know her. Wow, I met a sister when I was fifty-six years old.

I thank God for Aunt Shirley, Uncle Chuck, Aunt Dede, Mike, Kaye, Jon, and Liz. They have been wonderful, godly examples in my life. They have become a real family to me. I love them all very much.

As I mentioned earlier, I married a very special man.

He knew the story of how we had one night to pack when my sisters and I left Bethanna. He knew about my Mrs. Beasley doll. While visiting our daughter and her husband in North Carolina, we went to an antique store. I saw Mrs. Beasley in a box behind the cashier desk.

I was standing with my daughters and said to them, "Look there she is! My Mrs. Beasley doll!" I didn't know Michael was standing behind us. He bought her for me. What a loving surprise. He truly is the best.

Cindy and Michael

I once was told, "If you know the meaning of your name, you would try to live up to it."
Cindy—Shining light
Lou—Warrior

> In the same way, let your light shine before others, so that they may see your good works and give glory to your Father who is in heaven. (Matthew 5:16 ESV)

> For God gave us a spirit not of fear but of power and love and self-control. (2 Timothy 1:7 ESV)

Darn it all? Definitely not.
To God be the glory!
Thank you, Jesus!

About the Author

Cindy and her husband have been married since 1985. They were blessed with four beautiful children who are now adults with growing families. It brings her great joy to be able to spend time with all her grandchildren. Her family Pocono vacation is one of the best weeks of the year. She values and cherishes her family. In her spare time, Cindy enjoys cooking and tending to the vegetable garden in the summer. She enjoys blessing neighbors with meals and the bounty from the garden.